a gift for

from

OTHER GIFTBOOKS BY HELEN EXLEY:
Men! by women
A Spread of Over 40s' Jokes
Ms Murphy's Law
Women's Quotations
The Wicked Little Book of Quotes

OTHER BOOKS IN THIS SERIES
Too Soon for a Mid-Life Crisis
When I'm good I'm very very good – But when I'm Bad I'm Better!

Published simultaneously in 2004 by Exley Publications Ltd in Great Britain, and Exley Publications LLC in the USA.

12 11 10 9 8 7 6 5 4 3 2

ISBN 1-86187-590-8

A copy of the CIP data is available from the British Library on request.

Printed in China.

Exley Publications Ltd, 16 Chalk Hill, Watford, Herts WD19 4BG, UK.
Exley Publications LLC, 185 Main Street, Spencer, MA 01562, USA.
www.helenexleygiftbooks.com

Acknowledgements: The publishers are grateful for permission to reproduce copyright material. Whilst every effort has been made to trace copyright holders, we would be pleased to hear from any not here acknowledged. NAN TUCKET: From *The Dumb Men Joke Book* by Nan Tucket, published by Warner Books. PAM BROWN, PAMELA DUGDALE, CHARLOTTE GRAY, STUART AND LINDA MACFARLANE, MARGOT THOMSON: published with permission © Helen Exley 2004.

A HELEN EXLEY GIFTBOOK

a Woman's Work is never Done

Rowan Barnes-Murphy

The cock croweth
but the hen delivereth
the goods.

AUTHOR UNKNOWN

If you want a thing
well done,
get a couple of old broads
to do it.

BETTE DAVIS (1908-1989)

If you want anything said,
ask a man.
If you want anything done,
ask a woman.

MARGARET THATCHER, B. 1925

"A housewife is always in danger of meeting herself coming back"

PAM BROWN, B. 1928

Any mother could perform
the jobs of several
air traffic controllers with ease.

LISA ALTHER, B.1944

All mothers are physically handicapped.
They have only two hands.

AUTHOR UNKNOWN

My mother is very patient.
She would have to be with five kids,
four dogs and two jobs.

PAM REPEC, AGE 12

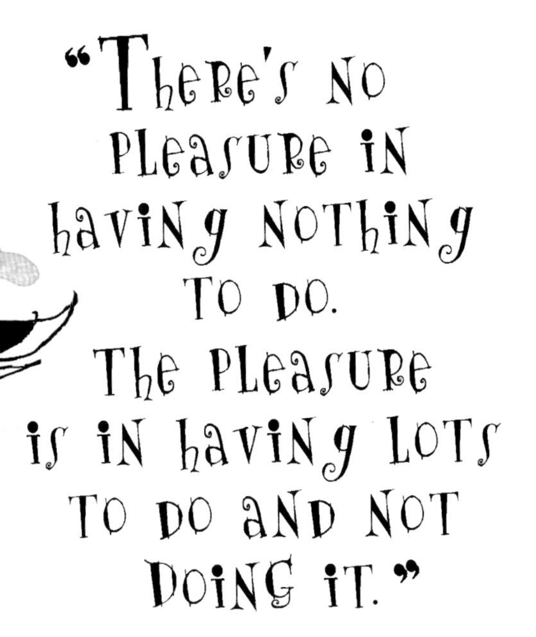

MARY WILSON LITTLE

I hate housework.
You make the beds, you do the dishes – and six months later you have to start all over again.

JOAN RIVERS, B.1933

"I don't like the terms 'housewife' and 'homemaker'. I prefer to be called 'Domestic Goddess' ...it's more descriptive."

ROSEANNE BARR, B. 1952

To be today's real woman,
you need to have the physique
of Venus, the cunning of Cleopatra,
the courage of Joan of Arc,
the wardrobe of Marie Antoinette,
and the cleaning ability
of Ammonia D.

JOYCE JILLSON

Love, Honour... and wash your floors

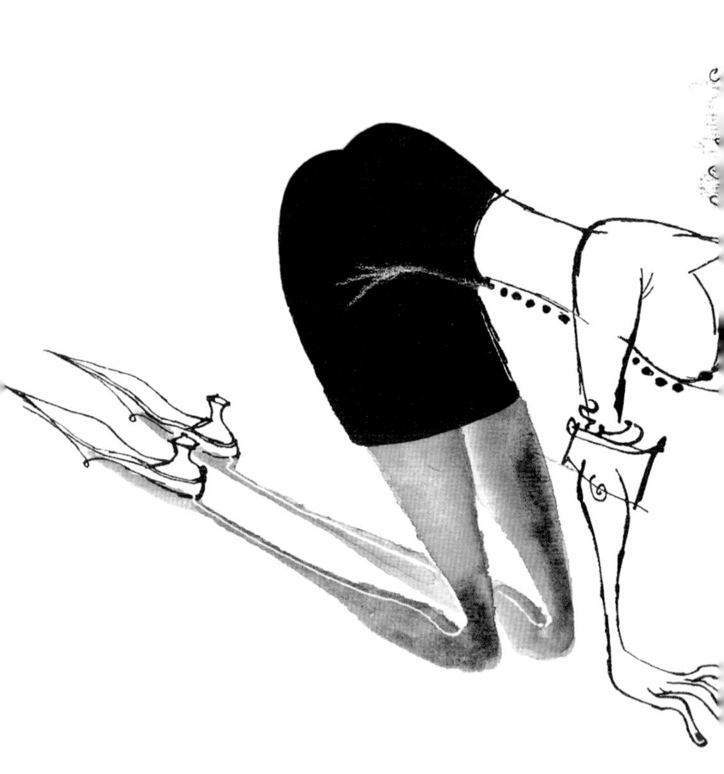

A girl becomes a wife with her eyes wide open. She knows that those sweetest words, "I take thee to be my wedded husband," really mean, "I promise thee to cook three meals a day for sixty years; thee will I clean up after; thee will I talk to even when thou art not listening; thee will I worry about, cry over and take all manner of hurts from."

ALAN BECK, FROM "WHAT IS A WIFE?"

HELPLESS SWEETIE

The natural woman loves and understands man far too well.... She knows... that without her he is a poor, weak, miserable, buttonless creature.

MRS. FANNY DOUGLAS

"Sometimes a husband would leave home if only he knew how to pack."

Margie Brand

"Modern drugs
are wonderful.
They enable a wife
with pneumonia to
nurse her husband
through flu."

JILLY COOPER, B.1937

BONE IDLE

A woman's work
is never done
– by men.

GRAFFITO

Before marriage,
a man will
lay down his life
for you; after marriage
he won't even lay down
his newspaper.

HELEN ROWLAND (1875-1950)

Men are like blisters.
They don't show up
until the work is done.

EDWARD PHILIPS

"How many men does it take to change a roll of toilet paper? We don't know, it's never happened."

Nan Tucket

(In his fridge) I found yogurt whose expiry date read "When dinosaurs roamed the Earth"

Kathy Lette, b. 1958

"A kinder God would have seen that mothers sprouted extra sets of arms with every birth."

PAM BROWN, B. 1928

All women have one gorilla arm.
That's the one we use to hold
the purse and the kids,
reach for the back zipper
and protect the front seat.

DIANE NICHOLS

The one thing children wear out
faster than shoes is parents.

JOHN J. PLOMP

LAZY LITTLE MONSTERS

A mother who
is going out rushes
round getting
everything ready
for when the family
comes home.
When she gets back...
she'll have to switch on
the microwave before
she gets her coat off.

CHARLOTTE GRAY, B.1937

Daughters are a delight.
Some of the time. Most of the time.
When, that is, they are not
putting their white ballet tights
into the wash inside black jeans.

PAMELA DUGDALE

Kids never believe their mum
has something she'd rather be doing
than washing their jeans.

PAM BROWN, B.1928

It puzzles me how a child
can see a dairy bar three miles away,
but cannot see a four by six rug
that has scrunched up
under their feet and has been
dragged through two rooms.

ERMA BOMBECK (1927-1996)

My mother is a lady
who has had a lot of problems
in her life.
Most of them me....

DIANA BRISCOE

Sometimes
she pretends not
to see me, when
I behave very badly.

CAMILLE FRASER, AGE 8

My mom is so busy
she has not got any hobbies
I suppose her hobby
is cleaning the house.

CRAIG, AGE 9

Cleaning your house
while your kids are still growing
is like shovelling the walk
before it stops snowing.

PHYLLIS DILLER, B.1917

There is this to be said
about little children:
they keep you feeling old.

JEAN KERR, B.1923

Mothers never get
their Big Night Out.
Someone always
comes out in spots
ten minutes before they leave.

PAM BROWN, B.1928

"I'M GOING TO CLEAN THIS DUMP JUST AS SOON AS THE KIDS ARE GROWN."

ERMA BOMBECK (1927~1996)

Getting your guy to help you

You can't change a man,
no-ways. By the time his
mummy turns him loose
and he takes up with
some innocent woman
and marries her,
he's what he is.

MARJORIE KINNAN RAWLINGS

A guy is a lump, like a donut.
So first you gotta get rid of
all the stuff his mom did to him.
And then you gotta get rid of
all that macho crap they pick up
from beer commercials.
And then there's my favorite,
the male ego.

ROSEANNE BARR, B.1952

How can you tell
when a man has insomnia?
He keeps waking up
every few days.

NAN TUCKET

What are three little words
you'll never hear a man say?
"I'll get it."

NAN TUCKET

I've been married
to one Marxist and one Fascist,
and neither one would
take the garbage out.

LEE GRANT

"If a man watches three football matches in a row, he should be declared legally dead."
Erma Bombeck
(1927~1996)
Z
Z
Z

To be able to turn a man
out into a garden
and tell him to stay there
until the next meal
is every woman's dream.

VIRGINIA GRAHAM

Give a man a fish and he eats
for a day. Teach him how to fish
and you get rid of him
for the whole weekend.

ZENNA SCHAFFER

Can you imagine a world
without men? No crime
and lots of happy fat women.

MARION SMITH

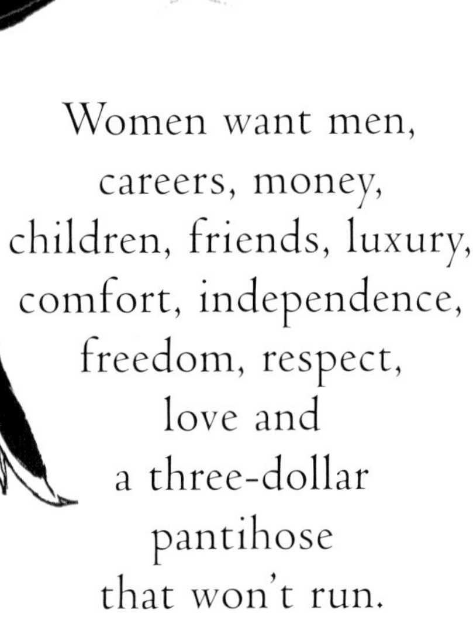

Women want men,
careers, money,
children, friends, luxury,
comfort, independence,
freedom, respect,
love and
a three-dollar
pantihose
that won't run.

PHYLLIS DILLER, B.1917

Kitchens, broom closets
and dust rags are not
in her dreams.

COLLEEN J. MCELROY, FROM "DAY HELP"

We Women...

"We women ought
to put first
things first.
Why should
we mind if men
have their faces
on the money,
as long as we get
our hands on it?"

Ivy Baker Priest

Do not be surprised when the sweet woman next door suddenly goes off to Kathmandu. She just washed his socks. One sock too many.

MARGOT THOMSON

Life is too short to stuff a mushroom.

SHIRLEY CONRAN, B.1932, FROM "SUPERWOMAN"

The fundamental reason that women do not achieve so greatly as men is that women have no wives.

MARJORIE NICHOLSON

"I would rather lie on a sofa than sweep beneath it."

SHIRLEY CONRAN, B. 1932

I believe in the total
depravity of inanimate things.
The elusiveness
of soap, the knottiness
of string, the transitory nature
of buttons,
the inclination of suspenders
to twist, and of hooks
to forsake their lawful eyes
and cleave only
unto the hairs of their
hapless owner's head.

KATHERINE ASHLEY (1840-1916)

"There comes a dreadful moment in our lives when foreign friends whom we strongly urged to visit us actually do so."

Virginia Graham

Is there anything worse than spending a night making strangers feel at home – which is precisely where you wish they *!!@* well were?

KATHY LETTE, B. 1958, FROM "MAD COWS"

I can't see the point in making tons of food if people are just going to sit there and eat it.

JENNY ECLAIR

If motherhood were advertized
in a job column, it would read:
"Hours – constant. Time off – nil.
All food and entertainment
supplied by you. No over-time.
No sick pay. No holiday pay.
No weekend leave. No pension.
Must be good at athletics,
home repairs, making mince
interesting and finding the pair
to the other glove.
Fringe benefits, none."

KATHY LETTE, B.1958, FROM "MAD COWS"

One moment makes a father,
but a mother is made by endless
moments, load on load.

JOHN G. NEIHARDT

MOTHERS SOMETIMES FEEL LIKE WEARING A PLACARD 'EVERYONE'S BUCK STOPS HERE'.

PAM BROWN, B. 1928.

Little Menace

Mommys are nice except when they find
gum sticking to their carpet.

MICHELLE, AGE 10

There are times when parenthood seems
nothing but feeding the hand that bites you.

PETER DE VRIES (1910-1993)

No matter what the critics say, it's hard
to believe that a television programme
which keeps four children quiet
for an hour can be all bad.

BERYL PFIZER

The quickest way for a parent
to get a child's attention is to sit down
and look comfortable.

LANE OLINGHOUSE

"I think children shouldn't be seen or heard."

JO BRAND

When all else fails, console yourself by saying, "It's just a phase."

H. JACKSON BROWN, JR.

"Of all the animals the boy is the most unmanageable."

PLATO (427–347 B.C.)

Boys pride themselves
on their drab clothing,
their droopy socks,
their smeared and inky skin:
dirt for them, is almost as good
as wounds. They work at acting
like boys. They... draw attention
to any extra departures
from cleanliness.

MARGARET ATWOOD, B.1939

"MEN LIVE UNDER THE DELUSION THAT A GOLD RING MAKES A WOMAN LIKE CLEANING WINDOWS."

PAM BROWN, B. 1928.

Among all the forms of absurd courage, the courage of girls is outstanding. Otherwise there would be fewer marriages.

COLETTE [SIDONIE GABRIELLE] (1873-1954)

A man loves a woman so much, he asks her to marry – to change her name, quit her job, have and raise the babies, be home when he gets there, move where his job is. You can hardly imagine what he might ask if he didn't love her.

GABRIELLE BURTON

There is an ancient cry among men, 'Sorry I just can't cope with sick'.
PAM BROWN, B. 1928

A man in love is so brave
that he can battle with fierce dragons,
but is not quite so brave
as to tackle the laundry.

STUART AND LINDA MACFARLANE

Men's inclination
for machine technology does not extend
to the washing machine.

PENNEY KOME

I blame Rousseau, myself.
"Man is born free," indeed.
Man is not born free, he is born
attached to his mother by a cord
and is not capable
of looking after himself for at least
seven years
(seventy in some cases).

KATHARINE WHITEHORN, B.1928

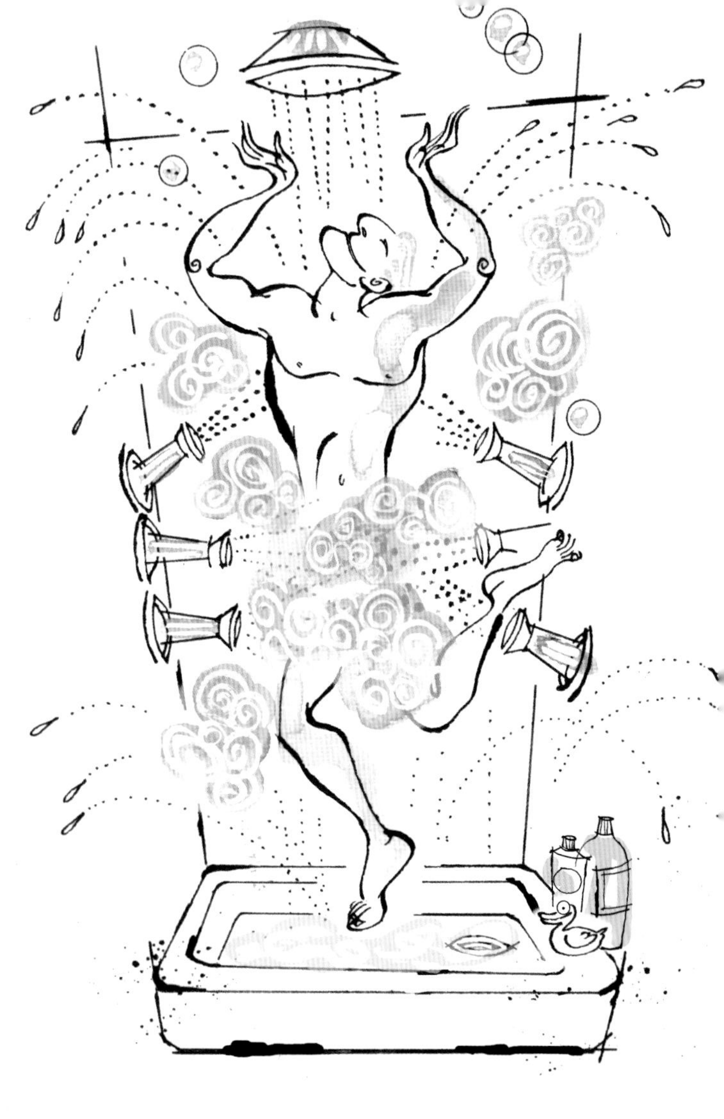

AUTOMATIC MESS MACHINES

. . .

Men never drip before getting out
of a shower. They saturate
themselves and then
plunge headlong into a towel –
leaving the bathroom
as though it's been through
a hard time in the North Sea.

PAM BROWN, B.1928

Why men are better than dogs?
Men only have two feet
that track in mud.

JENNIFER BERMAN,
FROM "WHY DOGS ARE BETTER THAN MEN"

What do you call
a man who
complains all day,
watches sport all night
and sleeps away
his weekends?
Normal.

NAN TUCKET

You can let off steam
to him and rant and rage,
and he'll look up
from his newspaper and say
"Did you say something dear?"

ANN WEBB

What's a man's idea of helping with housework?
Lifting his legs so you can vacuum.

NAN TUCKET

"No man has ever had an ordinary cold."

PAM BROWN, B. 1928

...it is impossible to rely
on the prudence or common sense
of any man...

MRS. ALEXANDER

A man's home may seem to be
his castle from the outside; inside,
it is more often his nursery.

CLARE BOOTHE LUCE (1903-1987)

WRITTEN IN 1589:
They are comforted by our means;
they are nourished by the meats we dress;
their bodies freed from diseases by our
cleanliness, which otherwise would surfeit
unreasonably through their own
noisomeness. Without our care they lie
in their beds as dogs
in litter and go like lousy mackerel
swimming in the heat of summer.

JANE ANGER, FROM "HER PROTECTION FOR WOMEN"
WRITTEN IN 1589

"Marry a man with a hobby and you get to clean the gear."

CHARLOTTE GRAY, B. 1937

Gardening men wash their hands
when they come in.
In the process of which
they transfer the mud to the basin,
the soap, the flannel
and the towel.
And leave it there as evidence
of the hard morning's work.

PAM BROWN, B. 1928

A man is the one
who has one sure-fire,
extra-special,
hey-presto recipe
which entails
a whole lot
of dirty dishes.

PAM BROWN, B.1928

When men cook, cooking is viewed
as an important activity;
when women cook, it is just
a household chore.

MARGARET MEAD (1901-1978)

...A WOMAN'S TOUCH

When a woman
has been down on her knees
scrubbing for
a week, and washing
for another week,
a man, returning
and finding his house
in order, and vaguely
conscious of a newer and
fresher smell about it,
talks quite tenderly of
"a woman's touch."

MAY SINCLAIR (1865-1946)

"If ever I get to Heaven, I'll be stuck making manna in the Holy Kitchens."

JILL TWEEDIE, B. 1936

Just as every human being believes he has a novel in him, so every uxorious husband believes his wife has a cookery book in her.

ALICE THOMAS ELLIS, B.1932

"If we can put a man on the moon, we can get rid of sports channel"

Nan Tucket

XX
XX
XX
XX

"I wanted to go out and change the world, but I couldn't find a babysitter."
Graffito

No animal is so inexhaustible
as an excited infant.

AMY LESLIE

A baby is an angel
whose wings
decrease as his legs
increase.

FRENCH PROVERB

I realize why women die
in childbirth – it's preferable.

SHERRY GLASER

When I got married,
I said to my therapist,
"I want to do something creative."
He said, "Why don't you have a baby?"
I hope he's dead now.

JOY BEHAR, B.1943

By the time the youngest children
have learned to keep the house tidy,
the oldest grandchildren
are on hand to tear it to pieces.

CHRISTOPHER MORLEY (1890-1957)

Women mean to do things,
go places, one of these days –
when the husband and kids
don't need them. By that
time they are probably too tired
to try!

PAMELA DUGDALE

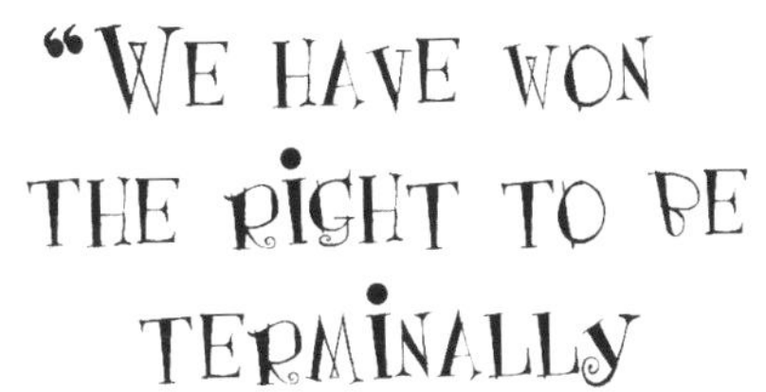

Erica Jong, b. 1942

HELEN EXLEY

Helen Exley has been collecting and editing material for her books for twenty-seven years and still enjoys complete involvement with each new title.

Her individually conceived and selected books have now sold fifty-six million copies since Exley Publications was formed in 1976. They are now found in thirty-nine languages on bookstalls as far apart as Delhi and Durban, Bridgetown and Santa Barbara.

ROWAN BARNES-MURPHY

Rowan Barnes-Murphy's cartoons are wicked, spiky and frayed at the edges.

His fantastically well-observed characters are hugely popular and have been used to advertise a diverse range of products such as cars, clothes and phones, supermarkets, bank accounts and greeting cards.

For more information contact:
Exley Publications Ltd, 16 Chalk Hill, Watford, Herts WD19 4BG, UK.
Exley Publications LLC, 185 Main Street, Spencer, MA 01562, USA
www.helenexleygiftbooks.com